Hope Street

Madness Defeated

I0117214

James Gerard McGinley
and John Sawkins

chipmunkapublishing

the mental health publisher

Published by

Chipmunkapublishing

PO Box 6872

Brentwood

Essex CM13 1ZT

United Kingdom

http://www.chipmunkapublishing.com

Copyright © James Gerard McGinley and John Sawkins 2012

Edited by Faith Mmadubuike

ISBN   978-1-84991-727-8

Chipmunkapublishing gratefully acknowledge the support of Arts Council England.

Contents

- **Introduction**

- **A pauper's guide to recovery - Susan C**

- **The Architect of Recovery - John Sawkins**

- **Unconditional Loving - Grace and Martin**

- **Changes - James Gerard McGinley**

- **Kaleidoscope - James Bishop**

- **What is hope?**

- **Compassion in action**

- **Making Recovery a Reality - Geoff Shepherd, Jed Boardman and Mike Slade**

- **Further Information and Contacts**

- **Conclusion**

Hope Street – Madness Defeated

Hope Street

"Had he been a stable and equable man, he could never have inspired the nation. In 1940, when all the odds were against Britain, a leader of sober judgment might well have concluded that we were finished," wrote Anthony Storr about Winston Churchill's bipolar disorder in Churchill's Black Dog.

Mental ill health, however, is not solely the property of the mentally ill. Just as the flu affects us all in different ways, and for varied periods of time, so does poor mental health.

There are too many variables to successfully diagnose and cure mental health problems in everyone overnight.

Hope Street focuses on lived experiences, coping mechanisms, endurance, hope and recovery.

In the past, recovery for most was only a dream. Today it has become a reality.

Health takes into account five parts; mental, physical, emotional, social and spiritual wellbeing. Equal consideration should be given to each part in order to maintain a healthy way of life.

Academic establishments tend to focus on a person's intellectual abilities and ignore a person's emotional abilities. As a result society does not have the tools to deal with problems such as teenage angst, bereavement, depression, anger, hate and a host of other emotionally- charged issues.

The good news is emotional intelligence can be taught.

With the appropriate training, support and help, most of us can learn how to cope. My advice would be to take some time out to become aware of your own stressors, triggers and needs.

Stress is the trash of modern life – we all generate it but if you don't dispose of it properly, it will pile up and overtake your life. ~ Danzae Pace

There are many paths to wellness when you are ill. Many search in vain for 'instant cures' when the answers already exist inside one's own being. As Bob Marley put it in Redemption Song: "emancipate yourself from mental slavery, none but ourselves can free our minds."

The recovery process is a personal journey that must be tailored to each individual's needs.

Hope Street focuses on five individuals who have had mental health setbacks and are now getting on with their lives. Most hold down full time jobs or meaningful activities and are stronger as a result of their experiences.

I use the mantra of 'pebbles in the dark' when I'm ill, breaking big tasks into smaller pieces, and giving myself more time to complete things. Sometimes you can achieve more by doing less, like the ripple effects of a pebble thrown into a pond.

The catalyst for change for me was the work of Dr. Viktor Frankl;

Adapted from Wikipedia;

Logotherapy was developed by neurologist and psychiatrist Dr. Viktor Frankl. It is considered the "third

Viennese school of psychotherapy" after Freud's psychoanalysis and Adler's individual psychology. It is a type of existentialist analysis that focuses on a "will to meaning" as opposed to Adler's Nietzschian doctrine of "will to power" or Freud's "will to pleasure".

The following list of tenets represents Frankl's basic principles of Logotherapy:

- Life has meaning under all circumstances, even the most miserable ones.

- Our main motivation for living is our will to find meaning in life.

- We have freedom to find meaning in what we do, and what we experience, or at least in the stand we take when faced with a situation of unchangeable suffering.

His book 'Man's Search for Meaning' (first published in 1946) chronicles his experiences as a concentration camp inmate and describes his psychotherapeutic method of finding meaning in all forms of existence, even the most sordid ones, and thus a reason to continue living. He was one of the key figures in existential therapy and was to become my first pebble, guiding me out of the dark.

James Gerard McGinley - BA Journalism

'There is no single definition of the concept of recovery for people with mental health problems, but the guiding principle is hope – the belief that it is possible for someone to regain a meaningful life, despite serious mental illness'.

Mental Health Foundation

Disclaimer - The posting of stories, commentaries, reports, documents and links (embedded or otherwise) in this book does not in any way, shape or form, implied or otherwise, necessarily express or suggest endorsement or support of any of such posted material or parts therein.

A Pauper's Guide to Recovery

To date I have not found any 'one reason' for my depression.

I know poverty plays a big part in my condition and there are a lot of things I still have to learn.

I don't suppose staying on my own in a less than suitable environment helps either.

Over the years, I have learned not to feed it or fight it, and I have noticed a steady improvement.

I have also developed a wealth of coping mechanisms for my dark days.

We are all different and react in different ways to different things. Through time, I have found out what stresses me and what triggers a depressive episode.

Oddly enough, I am cool and calm during a crisis.

There are things that you can never really plan for, however, like an unexpected bill or bereavement.

There is a whole list of small things I struggle with too e.g. I hate ironing, doing the dishes, or shopping when the shops are busy.

Mundane things drive me up the wall, though I know they are important.

In my wellness toolbox I have a free travel pass, my benefits, my friends, lots of books, a library card, a sports centre pass, an independent learning account, a computer, a phone, a cognitive behavioural therapist, a community psychiatric nurse, a set routine, medication and my voluntary job.

My family doesn't believe in depression, so I generally keep them at a distance when I am ill.

My social life is non-existent and my disposable income is next to nothing.

Depending on handouts for furniture and household appliances is tough.

Although depression has hindered me, it has also taught me a lot of lessons too.

Today, I'm a kinder person, I'm more humble and I certainly appreciate the little things I have got.

And I make my own clothes and jewellery.

To save money I do voluntary residential work and I have travelled all over and have made a lot of friends.

To get by and to keep busy, I do a few 'cash in hand' cleaning jobs.

But at the end of the day, I return to my nineteenth storey 'haven' in the sky all alone. I hate being alone. Sometimes I feel like Rapunzel waiting for her prince to come and save her.

Depression steals your spirit and cheats your mind. Assertiveness becomes non-existent and you become a passive receiver of anything dished out to you; good and bad.

In an ideal world, I would check into a health farm and work through all my 'stuff'.

I would learn how to take a holistic approach to health, mix with fellow 'sensitive' people and learn all sorts of life skills.

I would then return to the big city, or not, a new woman; given the choice I would prefer to live in the countryside.

As it is, I live in a multi-storey flat on an inner city housing complex.

The problems on the estate would fill ten books. Most people are poor, uneducated, but friendly and non-judgmental.

I do voluntary work on a little inner city farm.

Having regular contact with people and animals seems to help. It gives me a sense of purpose and a reason to keep going.

My books and music are a great escape too. I also like to watch movies with friends, though people tend to have little free time these days.

I don't think people avoid me because of my depression. My medical teams are the only people I really confide in.

I thought about getting a pet, but my housing association doesn't allow you to keep animals in the flats (despite the fact there are lots of 'animals' living here).

Sometimes I look at the lives of my friends and wonder what happened to me. I was always top of the class at school. Despite this, they all seem to be doing a lot better than me now.

How come? I often feel life just isn't fair.

When I'm really down I get a lot of strange thoughts and feelings. I have zero energy and something I call 'emotional toothache'. 'Please just take this pain away', is a constant thought.

I can't think clearly when I'm down and I often have suicidal thoughts too. It's at times like these I need to focus on the facts.

I have been here before and it will pass.

I can access my wellness toolbox for help and reassurance.

I am a beautiful person both inside and out (I struggle with this at times).

I'm worth more alive than dead.

There is so much more I want to see and do in life.

You never know what's around the next corner.

I am loved and love others.

I never make any big decisions when I am ill.

Also, I have placed pictures, poems and quotations all over my walls to remind me to be kind to myself and to keep my spirits up.

Being kind to others helps too.

Just spending an hour with my friend's children gives me a great boost. Unlike their parents, I am 'time rich' and 'cash poor'. The children really enjoy the time we spend together and it gives their parents a well earned break.

I have long since stopped asking 'why' and I now focus on 'how'.

How am I going to cope? And how am I going to accept myself as I am and move on.

I am aware that I must change and with the right support I will get there in the end.

I have read about so many women who have faced up to their fears and have gone on to live successful lives.

The J.K. Rowling story is an incredible example.

I am not looking for fame or lots of money.

All I want in life is to be comfortable and have a certain level of contentment. Anything else would be a bonus.

Hopefully, when I am ready, I will work up the courage to go to university.

I know so many people with mental health problems who have managed to get their degree with relative ease. Perhaps the problems come when you are forced back into the work place? Or perhaps some just take the wrong course?

An equal balance of practical knowledge and academic knowledge seems to be the way to go; hence my voluntary work with animals.

One day, I hope to become a vet. I love animals. I always have. There is a lot to be said for non-verbal communication.

This will be my third year working on the farm and I don't have any real debts as such.

The thought of debt really scares me. Over the coming year, I will enquire about the ins and outs of university.

Before I embark on my academic journey, I will make sure I have all the support I need to see the course through to the end.

As I have matured and admitted I needed help, more help has become available.

The more coping skills I have learned, the longer periods of wellness I have enjoyed.

Getting to sleep can take a while, and I know I can't function without at least eight hours rest.

For me recovery is more of a process. This process is easiest for me when I'm in a healthy routine.

Managing and monitoring all the different variables involved in my wellbeing has been made quick and simple with the use of an application on my mobile phone.

E mailing the resulting app-graphs to my doctor means that I don't have to visit the surgery quite as often. My CPN goes over the charts with me too.

My chemist takes my repeat prescriptions over the phone and delivers them to my door.

I was very passive when I first became ill. These days I demand only the best when it comes to my health.

A trip to America taught me all about the service industry and how it should be applied.

Unfortunately, word hasn't reached my home town of Glasgow yet and I can never really see good service being a general part of the culture here. Certain individuals and authority figures can be hard to deal with. Not everyone is rude and unhelpful, but sometimes it can save time and energy to get an advocate to do your talking for you.

Glaswegians in general are great. They remind me of big friendly bumblebees.

Is it possible to recover fully? I think there is a new generation of health services and technologies that are making the recovery process easier to navigate.

As more people go through this process and share their stories, it will offer hope to others.

To summarize, I would say I have recovered from many depressive episodes and have been well for long periods of time.

And if I manage to become a vet, work part-time, and get to live and work in the country, I will be the richest women alive.

Susan C

The Architect of Recovery

Architects rarely look back. They can live with the notion that they may well outlive their constructions. Once they have witnessed the realisation of some pet project, they have little more interest in it, preferring instead to concentrate on their latest idea. Change is a process that they embrace wholeheartedly. Like the architect, I had to teach myself to project my thoughts instead of replaying them. I learned to prefer new movies as opposed to reruns of old movies.

In order to escape from the domination of my past, I had to freeze-frame my experiences, and lock them away in a gallery. After all, memories are what make you the person you are, so you cannot pretend they did not happen. On the other hand, the brain is easily tricked: provided you furnish it with an image sufficiently vivid, it does not actually know whether this is fact or fiction, reality or fantasy. Visualisation techniques do work. False memories can be implanted. But I was content to preserve the genuine memories.

Next, I had to replace my worn-out gramophone records with some present day alternative, but I was not about to embark on the world of Second Life, or Face Book with its imaginary friends. No, for me, the way to move into the present was to occupy myself with creative pursuits, like music, art and creative-writing. Each of these is all-consuming. Because you are so engrossed in what you are doing, you do not have time to dwell on past disasters (or fears of future failures, for that matter).

And you do not have to be particularly proficient at any of these: it is the process, rather than the product that matters, though, of course, you cannot resist feeling somewhat proud of what you generate. I cannot paint for toffee, but I was determined to find some way of expressing myself through this medium, so I started teaching myself to use Corel Draw, a computer software package, which satisfied this need, (after overcoming the initial daunting phase, where the use of multiple layers and terminology can put you off).

I had taken an interest in what might loosely be called "abstract" art when I was at school, copying the style of Fernand Leger. The art teacher always encouraged us to depict a balanced composition; and to produce something that did not contain all the colours of the rainbow. He taught us to look through half-closed eyes, and to use our imagination, as well as what we could actually see. I got some of my "products" framed and I sold them, donating the proceeds to a local mental health charity.

My second venture into the unknown involved music, a subject which I had always enjoyed. However, I had only mastered the obligatory three chord trick on the guitar. Hence, joining the Big Band was, I felt, somewhat ambitious, particularly since I had agreed to play bass guitar, an instrument I had never played before! Nevertheless, as Johnny Ball would say, "You can do anything if you have enough confidence in yourself." Ten years later, I can just about busk my way through a Glenn Miller number, though I have to do it from memory, not being able to read the dots. (I did subsequently learn tab, which makes it easier, because you do not have to rely solely on your memory, which can occasionally let you down, particularly once you have a repertoire of over a hundred tunes). Using multi-tracking, I did eventually produce a passable CD, called iterative patterns, with thirteen songs that I had composed myself.

Finally, I tried my hand at another skill, writing. I could say that I had developed quite a good appreciation of the English language, having had every aspect of grammar drummed into me at the age of eleven, though its true relevance only struck me once I took up French, Latin and German, where conjugating verbs and declining nouns take on some actual significance. (There is an old David Frost joke about the Latin student, whose marriage was annulled, because, when asked to conjugate, he declined.)

So I started out by writing short stories and poems, settling eventually on the latter because I liked their ability to be concise (however obtuse or enigmatic they may appear to the reader). Eventually, however, I wrote a novel, which was ten years in the gestation, but took just six months in the writing.

All of these activities helped me to come to terms with, and manage my psychosis. Reading widely, and not just medical books and articles, helped me learn to understand my condition, and, as a consequence, appreciate the conditions of other people, too. This led in time to me acting as a volunteer advocate. It certainly helped me to empathise with clients, having "been there, done that and got the T-shirt".

So, you may well ask, if you so successfully learned to live in the present, gaining confidence and good health through such activities, why did you feel the need to try to become master of such a slippery time period as the future? In olden times, those that claimed to predict future events were condemned, once they joined the afterlife, to walk backwards to atone for the error of their ways.

However, I would argue that it is only when you actually make plans for future activities that you gain any control over your life. Without plans, you are condemned to be a victim. You become the passive recipient of actions imposed on you by others.

I had always been content to live from day to day, somehow fearful of anticipating possibilities too far ahead; but once I had embraced the notion of working a few months ahead and pencilling in future events in my diary, I began to realise how liberating this process was. Instead of relying on others to arrange the way my life was led, I was beginning to take back control, because it was now I who was choosing which events to attend. Indeed, I actually went one better and started putting on my own events, arranged months ahead.

The future, like reality itself, belongs to those who shape it, not to those who are content to accept someone else's idea of what it should be. If your vision is a strong one, you can make it happen. Those of us who are unhappy with the way psychiatric patients are treated cannot just sit back and complain: we must be prepared to do something about it. The power to change the medication, the system, or the world, for that matter, does not rest with the selected few, be they bankers, doctors or politicians – it is there for the taking, for everyone.

Of course, an individual can do little on his or her own: unity is strength, and communities can force change on the authorities. Nowadays, people use social media to create good effect.

Their power for good – as well as bad – has been witnessed in the so-called Arab Spring. Change is coming. Change is imminent. Let's be in the vanguard of it, so that we can participate in shaping it, rather than be shaped by it.

I don't need others to tell me how to manage my bipolar condition. I can do it for myself. I reached many of the same conclusions as the professionals' years ago. Recognising the triggers helps. Likewise the individual cycle. I know I will be feeling "flat" at Christmas, but I also know from experience that I will start to feel better by January, when the daylight returns, and I know that I will probably be at my most productive – if marginally hypomanic – by February. This phase, too, will pass and I will return to normal (whatever that is) in March, probably leading to another low on the chart by Easter.

It's all a bit like the economy, really. Bipolar, schizophrenia, etc: perhaps that is what the world is experiencing. Like many individuals, it is going through a deep depression. We have much to learn from economics: it's all one great big confidence trick. Whilst everyone believes things are going well, they keep the economy afloat by spending recklessly, like a hypomanic bipolar; but once the dreaded concept of fear rears its ugly head, the world, like the individual plunges into a deep depression.

This is where hope comes in. Barack Obama speaks of the Audacity of Hope. It takes a brave soul to be optimistic in the current climate, though we all know that only positive thinking can get us out of the economic mess this time. Hope liberates, where fear paralyses.

John Sawkins

Hope Street – Madness Defeated

Unconditional Loving

As I watched him sleeping, I knew I wanted to be with him forever. We had a strong spiritual bond and made a great team.

He was mentally and physically stronger than me, and at times it felt like he was my teacher.

There was a twelve year age gap between us, I was 18 years-old and he was 30 years-old.

Looks-wise, he was hot.

He did have a few flaws; his heart was bigger than his head, he loved everyone, except himself, unconditionally, and he kept a lot of things to himself.

We met in England on a working project for physically disabled people.

This was my year out and I really didn't want to fall in love with anyone.

After about two months, we left the project and went to live in his home town, Blackpool.

Before moving in together, he told me about his bipolar condition. Fortunately, my extended family back in the States had experienced mental health problems and I had an insight into mental ill health.

He had lived on his own for years and struggled with the idea of someone invading his space.

He was stubborn, fiercely independent, and the word compromise was alien to his being.

Though he was big and strong physically, his eyes looked scared. I sensed that he was in constant fear of another major mood swing; high or low. At first, he never really discussed recovery and what it meant to him.

I got a part-time job in a clothes shop and he went to college.

All of our disposable income went on travelling. Once a month we would hire a car and tour all over England.

Our life was very simple, but we were happy.

In a previous life, Martin was a policeman with good career prospects.

His illness was triggered by the death of his father. He had already lost his mother when he was five. Martin's father was his rock. When he died his whole world fell apart.

He wasn't the type to ask for help and withdrew into a deep depression for more than a year.

I wasn't there when Martin's world collapsed. His girlfriend dumped him, as did most of his so called friends.

The police services took care of him to a degree, but it was hard for Martin to move on and ultimately give up his job.

Not talking about mental health seems to be a very British thing. I'm not saying Americans are experts, but I think we are far more open. You guys see mental ill health as the end of the world. We see it as a need for change.

By the time Martin and I got together, he was pretty clued up on all aspects of mental health. He had read all the right books and subscribed to all the right charities.

He began to speak more about his hopes and desires for the future.

Our relationship was not centered on Martin's illness. He explained that even people with bipolar have 'normal' ups and downs.

We did discuss the things he struggled with and how he needed time on his own every now and then. To get a bit of an insight into his world I read Bipolar for Dummies. Martin said it was pointless reading too many books on the condition as everyone was different.

"We live in a labeling society. Get to know the person first, then the condition": said Martin.

He also said that being low was like trying to navigate through a swamp; frustrating, exhausting and thoroughly depressing.

When I asked him about being high he said: "When you are confident you think you can do anything. When you are manic, you know it."

To get a female's perspective I read 'An Unquiet Mind' by Kay Redfield Jamison. This explained a lot and gave me a real heads up on the condition.

Martin once told me about a discussion he and his father had.

His dad had told him: "Son, I'm very proud of you and all of your achievements. Now you're a man, I want you to start living for you."

These words didn't make much sense to Martin at the time, but they stuck with him.

When Martin began working with people with all types of disabilities, he couldn't believe just how much he got back in return.

His father's words of wisdom suddenly became clear. Martin was now living for himself and he loved it.

We spoke for hours about anything and everything. If we were about to argue we would stop, put on our jackets and head for the beach.

By the time we got back to the flat, we had sorted things out.

One night we were watching a movie and I burst out crying. I cried for almost one hour non-stop.

Martin just held me and said nothing.

When I was ready to speak, he made me a cup of tea. As it turns out I had been abused by a cousin when I was a child. For whatever reason, I had suppressed this whole period of my life.

Martin took me to his general practitioner who, following a five minute chat, prescribed Prozac. I was devastated. Martin explained that the GP didn't know me and didn't have access to my medical records. Prozac was all he could offer me as a short term solution.

The details of my abuse were too much for Martin to bear and he didn't feel qualified to deal with it.

What he did do was refer me to a female counselor who specialized in abuse. This was my preferred option, though it was really tough.

I attended hourly sessions every two weeks for about five months. Martin would meet me after each session. He never asked me about them.

He just cooked me a nice meal and we would go for a long walk that evening.

Back home my parents worried about me and I am sure my mother wanted me to marry a younger man.

Just as everything seemed to be back on track, Martin dropped a bombshell.

"I think you should go home", he said. "What?" I replied.

I really thought that this was the man I would marry and spend the rest of my life with.

Martin explained how he wanted to go to University and train to become a teacher. He told me that was a lot more opportunities in the States for me and how he didn't want me to miss out on the whole college experience.

Eventually we agreed on the compromise that we would spend holidays together.

What I didn't know then was that Martin would have married me in an instant. He just felt it was important to set me free for a few years in case I resented him in later life.

Or as he put it, "Grace the girl thinks she's in love. I just want to run it by Grace the woman too."

He also wanted space to work on his own feelings.

Even though Martin was med-compliant I didn't want to leave him.

We parted and kept in touch on the computer through Skype. He visited the States twice and I came back once.

After we had both finished university and college we decided to tour Europe.

I knew that this holiday could be our last, so I insisted we visit Paris; the city of love.

Martin took me to the restaurant in the Eiffel Tower. I was sure he was going to ditch me.

A waiter approached with a little parcel and gave it to me. I opened it to find an engagement ring.

"Grace, I have loved you since the first time I laid eyes on you. We have been on many journeys together. I think I can put up with your accent. Will you marry me?"

Those were his exact words!

"I'll think about it", I replied. Two glasses of wine later, I said yes.

We are now living in America and have two kids. Martin is a part-time teacher in the local junior-high school. He also takes care of our kids. He is a great dad and has the patience of a saint (He loves kids and doesn't find them stressful at all).

I became a lawyer just like mom and dad had always wanted (The money comes in handy too).

These days we still subscribe to mental health charities. We also golf, swim, hike and travel on a regular basis.

We have a strong circle of friends with children and similar interests.

Martin is fascinated by the American way of life. He loves the 'be all you can be mentality', but often re-words these slogans; 'reflect, then be all that you are'.

A lot of writers, actors, comedians and creative people have bipolar, but bipolar doesn't have them. Martin is still a big kid at heart. Being a father and teacher suits him.

The weather here has a lot less mood swings than the weather in the UK, so that helps too.

Over the years, we have learned a lot from each other and to this day we are still very much in love.

Grace

Kaleidoscope

Having been diagnosed with bipolar disorder about 9 years ago, I started on the complicated path of finding appropriate medical treatment. My wife Anna also started keeping a paper health journal so she could get a handle on what was happening.

In 2004, I took part in a 6-part education course at the Black Dog Institute in Sydney, for people with bipolar. It introduced me for the first time to the concepts of 'triggers' and 'wellness strategies'. This became a turning point on my journey. I changed my orientation towards my treatment; from being a passive recipient of medicines to an active participant in my own well-being. While medicine had always been the backbone of my treatment, I came to understand that to really 'live well' I needed to make other changes.

But with this new-found resolve, I soon became frustrated with the paper journal because I wanted to understand the 'data' better. Fortunately, I have an actuarial background which has served me well. Over time, I was able to convert my wife's mood diary into an Excel spreadsheet. Then I added charts, which helped me see the data and gave more clues as to what was going on with my health.

Slowly, some pieces of the puzzle began to fall into place e.g.

1. We used to have a busy social life. Through my diary, I began to notice that about 2 days after a meal out, I would spiral downwards very quickly and experience a period of depression for 5 or 6 days. It was a very strange but consistent pattern. I eventually discovered that certain food additives such as preservatives and artificial colors and flavors were triggers. This awareness allowed us to make changes in our lifestyle and upend our diets. I admit getting used to these adjustments was not easy, but on the upside, we pretty much eliminated one of my major triggers. It took us a couple of years to spot this pattern in my mood, and we would not have seen it without our handy spreadsheet.

Knowing my triggers continues to be very helpful. We have discovered the little things that can snowball, and we take appropriate action when these little things happen, or before they even start. It's a pre-emptive strike, so to speak. Whenever a trigger or potential trigger comes along, we have a specific plan to remove its effects. As a result, my depressive and manic episodes have become more intermittent.

Bipolar episodes are predictable: This realization is something that I've found to be true of myself but I don't think is widely believed. The key for me has been a deeper understanding of my episode triggers and the early signs and symptoms (i.e. cause and effect) that could start an episode. Armed with firsthand-knowledge of these interactions, I am now able to exercise better control over my mental health.

In fact, being able to methodically discover my triggers and stay well has changed my life so much that I turned my excel spreadsheet concept into a business. I never thought that having bipolar would turn out to be both a business venture as well as an opportunity for me to share helpful strategies on managing bipolar disorder; yet this is how things have turned out. And for that, I am truly grateful.

This isn't to say that I already have total control over my mental health.

But when I deteriorate or have an episode, it is most often due to a lack of self-control. I almost always know, or at least am fairly certain, of where I've gone wrong.

So is this all there is to it? Is staying well merely a result of knowing what makes you unwell? Reflecting on my own experience, knowing my triggers is one thing, but the motives for remaining healthy are just as important. Over the years, and even through great pain at times, I have resolved that there are several reasons for me to stay well. Here are those that top my list:

- Other people are better off when I'm well. My wife and kids are much happier and very relieved. I can communicate calmly with my business partners. I get on better with my parents and friends.

- Being depressed is miserable. Hypomania is great for a while – I get a lot of mowing done –

but it ends in misery too. For everyone, not just myself.

- When I'm well I'm physically healthier. I'm more sociable and people like me more.

- Being well costs less.

- I need to show my children what good mental health habits look like. I need to think of their psychological health too.

Surprisingly enough, there have also been good things that have come out of having bipolar. I've found that:

- I've learned how to say no. If you are good at something - work for instance - people ask you to do more. It builds up over time. So I've learnt to say, "No, I can't. I have bipolar. Sorry."

- I don't worry about what I'm going to wear, and I don't have to keep track of my clothes cycle. I don't care whether I need a bigger television or a new car. If I didn't have bipolar, these things might continue to consume me as they once did.

- My marriage is far stronger today than it would have been if I didn't have bipolar. My wife had enough reasons to leave me when I was ill for prolonged periods, but thankfully, she stayed even though she didn't understand what was wrong with me. Her perseverance has been a blessing to our marriage.

- I have great relationships with my kids and time with them is invaluable. Unfortunately, most dads don't spend more than a few minutes a day giving their kids undivided attention. Learning that I had bipolar was a good wake-up call. I now put more value on the people who are important to me, and that means giving those people more of my time.

- I've slowed down a lot. I stopped wearing a watch some years ago and haven't missed it. Losing track of time rarely causes problems. If I'm 10 or 15 minutes late for the doctor, it doesn't matter. He works to the same system anyway.

- I take my physical health more seriously than I used to. I'm frustrated by my lack of willpower to exercise, but the fact that I'm now more conscious about staying physically healthy is as good start as any – even if I can't always follow through with concrete action.

- I've always been very open about having a mental illness, and I've actually never felt the stigma that is so widespread. I'm fortunate in that respect. When I converted to Christianity about 20 years ago I lost most of my "good" friends who had an issue with it. Since I've been telling people that I have bipolar I've gained at least the same number. Go figure.

- I've learned to be thankful for what I have and not yearn for what I don't.

- I've gained the ability to empathize with others who are facing the same problems.

While having bipolar disorder has been a challenge for me and my family, it has not been an insurmountable one. I never imagined I would live to see the day when I would look on my condition as more of a blessing than a bane, but that is exactly where I am at this point in my life.

Before being diagnosed with bipolar, I thought my life was over. But the diagnosis itself brought my wife Anna and I great relief; because we knew what we were dealing with and could start working on it. Today, I see my situation as an ongoing learning process and a kaleidoscope of opportunities.

James Bishop, Sydney, Australia

Changes

The past twenty three years have been like a rollercoaster ride and I have been hospitalized countless times in conditions you would not believe.

When I first became ill in 1988 there was no support in the community for people with mental health problems. If you couldn't function or were a danger to yourself or other people, you would be locked up and heavily sedated in a psychiatric unit.

The first institution I was incarcerated in was Woodilee Lunatic and Pauper Asylum.

Opened 1875, Closed 2001

It was a terrifying experience. I can only equate the conditions to that of the Nazi death camps where prisoners were rendered powerless, stripped of all dignity and pride in sub-human conditions.

I was in a bad way and needed help. Unfortunately, so was the world of psychiatry.

It all happened so quickly and I wasn't really sure what was going on. The unit was situated in the suburbs of Glasgow miles away from my family home.

The deafening shrill of crows echoed through the tree-lined driveway that led to the main building. I was petrified, but tried not to show it. There was no welcoming sign at the entrance, just the bold words **'ASYLUM'** engraved on the old Victorian institution's wall.

Following a rushed medical and a brief question and answer session, they told me to strip and handed me a pair of State pyjamas. I glanced through a small window on the door and was horrified to see a gathering of inmates waiting eagerly to greet me.

Entering the ward was like Dorothy's arrival into a sinister Oz-hell. In front of me were dozens of strange looking creatures chattering away in a language I could not understand.

Most had horrific physical scars and wasted no time telling me this is how I would end up.

The ground floor building had barred windows and an outside door that was always locked. There was a row of around twenty beds facing another twenty; privacy was non-existent. The smell was nauseating and the toilets were repulsive.

Initially, I was scared, humiliated and angry. I was also lost and puzzled as to why I had ended up in such an appalling place. I couldn't understand why I was being punished for being ill?

Just seven days earlier it was all so different. There was I, your archetypal yuppie; a sharp, confident, 23 year-old with lots of friends, a good job, girlfriend, not bad looks and a strong physique.

This was the last place I needed to be to sort myself out.

My whole being went into survival mode. I had to learn the ways of the unit and do my 'time' the best I could.

A typical day would start at 8am. Some would rise before this, rummaging through bins for old cigarette butts to calm their rattling nerves.

Once you had made your bed, you were frog-marched into the bathroom for a shave, shower or bath. At all times you were under the watchful eyes of the guards.

Mostly these were big strong men who took no nonsense. You did as you were told, or suffered the consequences.

Following this, you were led to the canteen where you dined with the female inmates.

One morning the unit's boss came into the dining room. I looked at my watery porridge and thought about confronting him about the overall conditions.

I only took about three steps in his direction when two guards pounced on me, pinned me to the floor and dragged me outside

After breakfast you were given the drug Largactil. It had different effects on each inmate. Some would turn into zombies. Some would hide and sleep under beds. Some would try to sleep on chairs. And some of the more experienced inmates would ask for the tablet form and simply spit it out in the toilet.

Next, the whole ward had to be cleaned from top to bottom.

You were under strict orders not to lie or sit on your bed during the day; if you had too much rest you would keep the night shift staff up.

So, from eight in the morning to eight at night, the only thing to do was pace up and down the ward, or look out of the windows. As you can imagine, the days were long and boring.

There was no safe place to store possessions; so you had to keep your wits about you at all times

Fights and theft were common place. The staff would deal with this by jumping on inmates, injecting them with a sedative, and locking them up in a specially secured padded cell.

When 8pm came, I would pull my curtains closed and enjoy a little bit of privacy. My shoulders would fall slightly and I would drop my guard and relax a little.

Putting so many strangers together in such a tight environment, for such a long period of time, was just asking for trouble.

Looking back, I think my naivety was a good thing; I wasn't aware just how dangerous the other inmates were, or why they had been incarcerated.

A bucket-load of tears was shed by me, my family and my friends when they locked me up in that place. I received no therapy, resolved no issues, and was left with a bitter taste of anger and mistrust towards the medical profession as a whole.

After about ten weeks, they sent me home shattered and broken with no grounds for appeal.

This was when I was at my lowest. Most of my days were spent sleeping on my dad's sofa wishing I was dead.

The memories of the psychiatric unit were still really clear in my head and haunted me day and night. It was more than a year before my mood began to lift. I had no job, no girlfriend, with the label of someone who was partial to a wee bit of mental illness.

I had no idea of who I was, where I was going, why I had suffered a breakdown, or how to make things better. Having been ill for so long, I was desperate to get away.

I have always thought that it is hard to get a clear view of your life when you are in the middle of it. I needed a bit of time out in a suitable environment to reflect.

"The road of life twists and turns and no two directions are ever the same. Yet our lessons come from the journey, not the destination."

Don Williams, Jr. (American Novelist and Poet)

On my return, it became clear that I needed help to manage my condition. I set up a charity called 'Time Out' and hoped it would take off. It was a great success and even won a few awards. Speaking to people who had 'been there' was such a relief.

I learned about money, benefits, budgeting, and paying all my bills via direct debit. We brought in speakers and completed worldwide research.

In time, I learned how to take responsibility for my condition, identify triggers, identify stressors, and other self-management techniques (see www.findingoptimism.com).

The true power of the group was the group.

Slowly, I was putting myself back together. More mental health charities were being formed and it seemed like Scotland was beginning to pay more attention to mental health.

My subsequent degree in journalism was partly inspired by my time on those barbaric wards. My degree is now a powerful tool that helps me communicate more effectively.

"There can be no higher law in journalism than to tell the truth and shame the devil"

–Anon

As a writer I've started to look at my condition as a gift. I know that sounds strange, but it gives me a different perspective compared to other writers. I've also adopted the trendy 'keeping it real' motto and now practice Tai

Chi; the philosophy of which is just 'common sense and going with the flow'.

I still have my highs and lows like everyone else. However, these days I try to have a good balance in everything I do, including a healthy food regime. To be honest, I really don't think I would be this health conscious if I hadn't encountered mental illness.

My anger towards medical professionals has long since passed and I now have a community psychiatric nurse whom I trust, an occupational therapist who keeps me on my toes, and a top psychiatrist whose wisdom and grace far outweigh her years.

"Knowing others is intelligence; knowing yourself is true wisdom. Mastering others is strength; mastering yourself is true power." – Anon.

On the left is the Old Gartnavel Royal Asylum where I spent many days suffering in silence; as an inmate you didn't really have a voice.

On the right is the new Garnavel Royal Hospital where I have only spent three days to date. The new hospital has single occupancy en suite rooms, a restaurant, a TV room, a therapy room and mentors that were former patients. There is now a whole range of prescription drugs and therapies on offer.

Psychiatrists, nurses, patients, charities, and even governments all over the world are coming together to promote recovery. It's a slow process and there is still a lot of work to be done. More educational psychologists are needed in the NHS, our schools, universities and places of work.

General practitioners need help to tackle the root causes of mental ill health and not just the symptoms.

Authorities such as the police, housing associations, and law makers need to gain a better understanding of mental health.

A sprinkling of compassion and respect throughout society would help too. And finally, individuals must take responsibility for their own wellbeing and make healthy living a priority.

My medical team, in football terms, was once a bankrupt third division side. Now, with me as manager, they are Barcelona; European Champions.

On my journey, I have learned that petty bickering and hate achieves nothing, and that education, empathy, forgiveness and compassion achieve results.

I have always had hope in my life, but just didn't see it (sometimes I can be a bit slow). Fear and confusion has kept me back for a long time. Today, that fear has gone and I am learning more about the recovery process. The power of nature helps revitalize my spirit and music helps feed my soul.

Given the appropriate support, I hope to return to University, and perhaps even part-time work one day. My medical team will tell me if and when I am ready.

And as a new member of the Royal College of Psychiatrists' Service Users' Recovery Forum, I can share hope with others and help promote sustainable recovery.

James Gerard McGinley

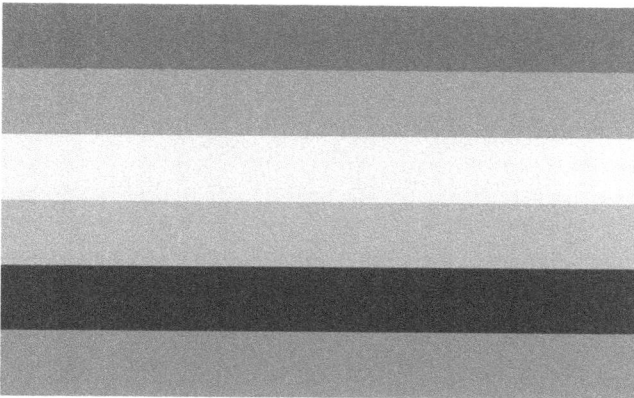

What Is Hope?

Adapted from Wikipedia:

Hope is the emotional state which promotes the belief in a positive outcome related to events and circumstances in one's life. In the English language the word can be used as either a noun or a verb, although hope as a concept has a similar meaning in either use.

Hope in Psychology

One psychologist argues that hope comes into play when our circumstances are dire, when things are not going well or at least there's considerable uncertainty about how things will turn out. She states that, "hope literally opens us up and removes the blinkers of fear and despair and allows us to see the big picture, thus allowing us to become creative and have belief in a better future."

Psychologist, C.R. Snyder and his colleagues say that hope is cultivated when we have a goal in mind, determination that a goal can be reached, and a plan on how to reach those goals. Hopeful people are, "like the little engine that could, because they keep telling themselves, "I think I can, I think I can".

Hope is distinct from positive thinking, which refers to a therapeutic or systematic process used in psychology for reversing pessimism. The term 'false hope' refers to a hope based entirely around a fantasy or an extremely unlikely outcome.

"Simplicity is the ultimate sophistication"

Leonardo da Vinci

Compassion in Action

Recently, I attended a training course on Compassion Focused Therapy. I chose to attend this as I was curious about how it could benefit people that I work with and how it could help me in my own life. It was a real eye-opener for me as a person and also in my practice as a mental health nurse.

So what did I learn?

Firstly, I thought I knew what the meaning of compassion was. In reality, I did not fully embrace its true therapeutic benefits.

I often got caught up in having to do things for my patients rather than just 'being' with them.

As a mental health nurse, I have often witnessed people's pain and have felt powerless to help them.

This led me to question my ability as a nurse; whatever I did was never quite good enough. Germer (2009, page 33) describes this very succinctly when he states:

"In emotional life, the sooner we stop struggling to fix things, the better. Paradoxically, then, care leads to cure."

Germer (2009: page 33) also describes what being compassionate means:

"When we offer genuine compassion, we join a person in his or her suffering. Being compassionate means that we recognize when someone is in pain, we abandon our fear of, or resistance to it and a natural feeling of love and kindness flows toward the suffering individual."

These points are crucial to a mental health nurse's role in helping patients on the road to recovery.

So how do we do this?

I began by attending a training course on compassion focused therapy.

At first I struggled with the practice of CFT. The instructor then asked me to imagine someone who meant a lot to me and then to direct compassion towards them. This part wasn't so difficult, however, when I was asked to show compassion to myself, that was a different matter.

It took a while, but once I learned just 'to be' in the moment the floodgates opened; I had connected with me. It was a very profound and moving experience. And it is the first training course I have been on which was so accepting of emotions and where I didn't feel judged.

".... to turn inward and give to ourselves the love, understanding and forgiveness that can make us whole. The compassion for others comes then from this strong, fulfilled sense of oneself."

Sandy Boucher (1997: page 127) in her book Opening the Lotus

I now practice the skills of compassion, mindfulness and soothing breathing rhythm on a daily basis. I can now see and feel many improvements in me; I feel different, I am much gentler to myself and to others around me, I am less quick to judge and I am much calmer.

It is only now that I can truly say that I will be able to pass on these skills and hopefully my patients and I will travel the road to recovery together.

Jackie McTaggart, NHS, Mental Health Nurse and Clinical Researcher

Making Recovery a Reality

Recovery has been defined as 'a way of living a satisfying, hopeful and contributing life even with the limitations caused by illness. Recovery involves the development of a new meaning and purpose in one's life as one grows beyond the catastrophic effects of mental illnesses'.

In Making Recovery a Reality, we set out what we believe are the key themes of recovery:

1. Agency - gaining a sense of control over one's life and one's illness. Finding personal meaning - an identity which incorporates illness, but retains a positive sense of self.

2. Opportunity - building a life beyond illness. Using non-mental health agencies, informal supports and natural social networks to achieve integration and social inclusion.

3. Hope - believing that one can still pursue one's own hopes and dreams, even with the continuing presence of illness. Not settling for less, i.e. the reduced expectations of others.

A new rationale

Recovery is an idea whose time has come. It provides a new rationale for mental health services and has radical implications for the design and operation of mental health services and partnerships between health, social services and third sector organizations.

The closure of the large institutions, the development of community-based services and policy initiatives which emphasize recovery all provide opportunities to make recovery orientated practices and services integral to the organization and delivery of mental health services.

Geoff Shepherd, Jed Boardman and Mike Slade

Download free from the website: www.scmh.org.uk

"The only mark of perfection is to tolerate the imperfections in others." – Anon.

'Weave some Hope through Life'

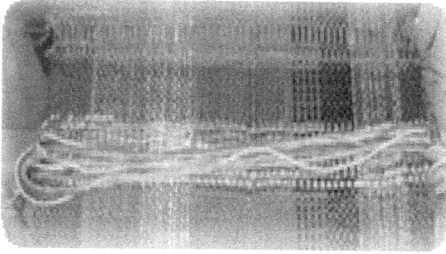

Royal College of Psychiatrists
17 Belgrave Square
London SW1X 8PG

www.rcpsych.ac.uk

Black Dog Institute

The Black Dog Institute is an educational, research,
clinical and community-oriented facility offering
specialist expertise in mood disorders.

Hospital Road
Prince of Wales Hospital
Randwick

Australia NSW 2031

www.blackdoginstitute.org.au

What is emotional intelligence?

The term Emotional Intelligence (EI) is a relatively new one. It has been popularised by Daniel Goleman, originally a science journalist now a consultant / academic at Rutgers University Graduate School in New Jersey. Goleman defines EI as:

knowing what you are feeling and being able to handle feelings without having them swamp you;

being able to motivate yourself to get jobs done, be creative and perform at your peak; and sensing what others are feeling, and handling relationships effectively

It is, in other words, that critical group of non-cognitive skills, capabilities and competencies, which help someone, control and manage their emotional response to events and pressures.

www.managementcentre.co.uk

Scottish Recovery Network
Suite 320-323 Baltic Chambers
50 Wellington Street
Glasgow G2 6HJ

www.scottishrecovery.net

Working to Recovery
28 Habost, Port of Ness
Isle of Lewis, HS2 0TG
Tel: (44) 01851 810060

www.workingtorecovery.co.uk

Optimism Apps Pty Ltd

With the emphasis in healthcare moving towards preventative care, effective computer based technologies are ideal for delivering low cost treatments. In this context, mental health software company Optimism Apps Pty Ltd has developed a suite of popular mood chart and health planning applications for use by mental health professionals and individuals.

James Bishop Optimism Founder
Suite 1, 461 High Street
Penrith NSW 2750
Australia

www.findingoptimism.com

Mary Ellen Copeland
Mental Health Recovery and WRAP (Wellness Recovery Action Plan)
PO Box 301
W. Dummerston, VT 05357

www.mentalhealthrecovery.com

Recovery Devon is a community of people supporting mental health recovery and wellbeing. The group works in partnerships to promote the philosophy and practice of recovery oriented approaches to support improved mental health and wellbeing. (The Department of Health, Melbourne, Victoria, Australia has recently published an excellent Framework for recovery-oriented practice. This is aligned very closely with the philosophy of recovery as we understand it in Britain – for more information check out Recovery Devon's website).

www.recoverydevon.co.uk

Making Recovery a Reality written by Geoff Shepherd, Jed Boardman and Mike Slade.

Download for free from the website; www.scmh.org.uk

Aware

Their mission is to create a society where people with depression and their families are understood and supported, are free from stigma and have access to a broad range of appropriate therapies to enable them to reach their full potential.

National Office

72 Lower Leeson Street, Dublin 2.

www.aware.ie

Carers UK

Information and help for the UK's six million carers.
Tel: 020 7490 8818
Carers line: 0808 808 7777
info@carersuk.org

www.carersuk.org

HandsOnScotland

HOS is an online resource for anybody working with children and young people. They provide practical information and techniques for developing positive mental wellbeing.

Rethink

Founded almost 40 years ago, giving a voice to people affected by mental illness, their families, carers and friends. They offer advice and information, support and understanding, help and hope.

www.rethink.org

World Federation for Mental Health
12940 Harbor Drive, Suite 101
Woodbridge, VA 22192
USA

www.wfmh.org

Mental Health Foundation

MHF are committed to reducing the suffering caused by mental ill health and to help us all lead mentally healthier lives. MHF help people to recover from and prevent mental health problems.

'Spirituality can help people maintain good mental health. It can help them cope with everyday stress and can keep them grounded'.

www.mentalhealth.org.uk

DREEM (Developing Recovery Enhancing Environments Measure)

DREEM is an outcome measure and research tool to see how 'recovery-oriented' a service is. It is a self-report instrument that gathers information about mental health recovery from people who are using mental health services. The DREEM asks people where they are in their process of mental health recovery and what markers of recovery they are currently experiencing.

You can find out more about DREEM on the Recovery Devon website: www.recoverydevon.co.uk

Recovery Star

This is tool for people using services to enable them to measure their own recovery progress, with the help of mental health workers or others. The 'star' contains ten areas covering the main aspects of people's lives, including living skills, relationships, work and identity and self-esteem. Service users set their personal goals within each area and measure over time how far they are progressing towards these goals. This can help them identify their goals and what support they need to reach them, and ensure they are making progress, however gradual, which itself can encourage hope. You can find out more about Recovery Star on the Mental Health Providers Forum website: www.mhpf.org.uk/index.asp

Universal Comedy

Founded in 2004, UC deliver comedy workshops and training courses for people experiencing the downside of ill health, depression and anxiety, employment problems or anyone who would benefit from a laugh
Finnieston House (Ground Floor)
9 Argyle Court
1103 Argyle Street
Glasgow G3 8ND

www.universalcomedy.co.uk

Centre for Confidence and Well-being

www.centreforconfidence.co.uk

The Centre can now only be contacted by email:
contact@centreforconfidence.co.uk

Living Life to the Full – A free online resource that teaches life skills

The content of the LLTTF site is written by Dr Chris Williams, a well-known CBT trainer and teacher.
www.llttf.com

International Video Clips on YouTube

The Recovery movement; a 2009 lecture by Myra Piat Part 1

www.youtube.com/watch?v=ZaA-Dx9okXQ&feature=related

Implementing recovery in mental health; a US perspective Part 1 what is recovery?
www.youtube.com/watch?v=3re1KvUlGFs&NR=1

The Arts

Movie Clip

From The Shawshank Redemption depicting Hope:

www.youtube.com/watch?v=hWUfFwoe8ko

Dance

People reveal how dance has been a powerful tool in their recovery from mental health problems.

www.communitychannel.mediatrust.org/video/XmBnlG5ghLl/

Music

This is powerful: Stigma
www.youtube.com/watch?v=vaY5PzX2eEo&feature=rel
ated

Also, check out the Media Trust website:
www.mediatrust.org

Books

Ekhart Tolle's message is simple: living in the now is the truest path to happiness and enlightenment. And while this message may not seem stunningly original or fresh, Tolle's clear writing, supportive voice and enthusiasm make this an excellent manual for anyone who's ever wondered what exactly "living in the now" means. Foremost, Tolle is a world-class teacher, able to explain complicated concepts in concrete language. More importantly, within a chapter of reading this book, readers are already holding the world in a different container--more conscious of how thoughts and emotions get in the way of their ability to live in genuine peace and happiness.

Tolle packs a lot of information and inspirational ideas into *The Power of Now*. (Topics include the source of Chi, enlightened relationships, creative use of the mind, impermanence and the cycle of life.) Thankfully, he's added markers that symbolise "break time". This is when readers should close the book and mull over what they just read. As a result, *The Power of Now* reads like the highly acclaimed *A Course in Miracles*--a spiritual guidebook that has the potential to inspire just as many study groups and change just as many lives for the better. *--Gail Hudson*

Ruyard Kipling
IF – Poem
Jungle Book – Movie and book

Helping CDs

Louise L. Hay – www.LouiseHay.com

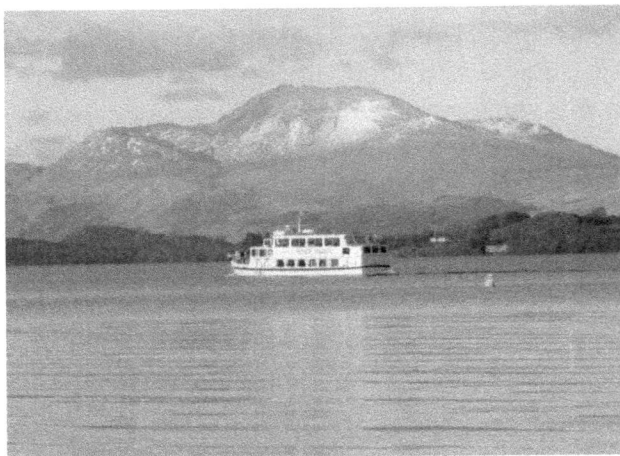

Hope Street

The stories, contacts and research in this book have shown that recovery is now possible.

We have embarked on an inspiring global journey that has given us an insight into different mental health environments.

The real experts in the field of mental ill health, the users, have given us simple recovery tips in a clear language that we can all understand.

The directions they have given us will help, but our personal journeys will be unique.

Fear, lack of support, mistrust, poor communication and lack of planning have hindered the recovery process in the past.

People who have been marginalised by society for so long are now standing up for their rights and are playing important roles in determining their own future and the future of others e.g. as mentors in psychiatric hospitals and as members of committees like the Royal College of Psychiatrists' Service Users' Recovery Forum.

It is no secret that the world of psychiatry has a chequered past involving scores of horror stories.

We must not forget the past, but learn from it and move on.

Some countries still have very poor mental health systems. As we improve our own, we must not forget those most in need.

Mental health is a fast moving industry with many parts e.g. health care professionals, pharmaceutical companies, carers, users, self-help groups, charities and many more.

When all of these parts work in harmony, they form a solid foundation for the recovery process.

(I have often wondered what would happen to the mental health industry if an 'instant cure', similar to laser eye surgery, was discovered).

Stigma is still a problem in the mental health world and as a progressive society we must do our best not feed it, or make it easy for people to stigmatise.

Rightly or wrongly, young people in need of support are extremely image conscious. Following a diagnosis, they are more likely to join a support group that will educate and support, not label them further.

It is important to realize that we are all individuals with different needs. Time Out, the charity I founded, had no labels. We met in a hall with no attachments.

Everyone was welcome and we had no barriers for those of different beliefs, sexual orientation, or age. Blanket labeling and gross generalizations were not for us.

It sometimes helps when prominent members of society come forward and talk openly about their mental health experiences; giving others the confidence to do the same.

Suicide is far too big a problem to discuss here. When I am down I try stick to the facts, as depression distorts a clear frame of mind. It is not wise to make any big decisions when you are ill. For me, suicide is a permanent solution to a temporary problem. With the right help, anything can be sorted out.

The people I have met while putting this book together have inspired me, shown me the importance of a structured routine and how to achieve a healthy balance in all aspects of my life.

More and more people around the world are coming to live on Hope Street; hence taking the first steps towards recovery.

The writers involved in this book have bravely come forward to inspire others. Their message is simple: 'There is always Hope'.

"Mental ill health has finally come out of the cauldron of madness and can now be seen for what it really is; a perfectly normal part of life."

James Gerard McGinley - BA Journalism